Frig!d

The Existential Adventures of a Spinster

Jessica Page Weber

BookLeaf Publishing

India | USA | UK

Made with ❤ on the BookLeaf Publishing Platform
www.bookleafpub.in
www.bookleafpub.com

Dedication

This poetry book, "Frig!d: The Existential Adventures of a Spinster," is dedicated to those who embrace modern poetry with an open heart and a curious mind.

And, to those who believe that the world is a canvas, painted with the vibrant colors of adventure and wonder, may each day offer a new opportunity to uncover hidden treasures, life and health.

To the readers of this book, remember that every path, no matter how well-trodden, holds the potential for something magical if we only dare to explore it.

With gratitude and hope that these pages bring you as much joy in reading as I found in writing them,

Lifting up The Impressionists -- The Manets and Monets!

Jessica

Preface

The idea for "Frig!d" was not easy -- it was formed. I changed, and altered poetry left and right, and write and write, and thought and turned for 21 days and more. This book is a celebration of that spirit.

Thank you for joining me on this journey.

Warm regards,

Jessica

Acknowledgements

To my lovely, wonderful teachers and professors — thank you!

And to my immediate family who always reads some poetry at Christmas ... — you know who you are, ;)

0. Millions of us enter a room everyday...

Millions of us enter a room every day and look at ourselves only. Midlife is not a new territory though - it is one that has been traveled before - by many hopers, dreamers, seekers, kind souls and friends of the world. Many divorcees have said that they have felt midlife more than the spinsters or those in single life, but how is that a new scene? If we all sit down and take a good look at our heart, what do we get? Do we get a summation of life experience in a small nano-second of coffee chat? Or, do we sit down and forget in front of the television with our dog? Or, do we not even consider as we run to the gym and pump out steps, beats, and weights? Do we call our family and ask of them? What do we get? "Woof." Wait, there's Barkley --- so stable.

1. Ice Cube (Free-verse)

Barkley eats three meals a day if he wants.
Picky, picky, pridefully, painfully, picky.
If the morsel is small,
the dog will fill his tummy,
the day will be easy 4 dog-mummy.
First, it was Purina, then Purina canned, then Purina
other, then Purina moist, it was never ending.
Then, Purina only-chicken-flavor and no vegetables for
Barkley.
Oh, what a good eater this Barkley isn't?
Oh, but He listens so well.
Plop.

2. Confusion of Being.

O - Obvious annoyances always exist.

F - Feeling sick means many things.

B - Being a good person is similar to a few things.

E - Exiting the day is a lesson.

I - I think, therefore I am; I am - therefore I am?

N - Never underestimate.

G - Gee, it's hard to tell. Ending the day with a prayer is good.

3. Freezer (Free-verse)

Don't play in the park.
Running, ruley, rule-based, riding, rustling, rough.
The day is hot & wet,
To care for ourselves is so important and animals are
part of that.
Eat and pray.
Love and be kind.
The idea of waiting is a task worth-understanding.
Watch the daily tasks kick in every day!
It is so similarly repetitive.
Yazoo.

4. A Dog's Dictionary

DOG, abbreviation for your favorite animal

DOG, /dug/ (L dog, to rule the house)
1. Exerting love in domicile
2. Exerting presence in domicile

DOG, a canine theorist on life, parks and heeling

DOG, a comfort that incorporates animal and human connection and barking

DOG, that third possible presence in the shopping cart

DOG, once in a life companion

DOG, a situation in which role and expectation does not change

DOG, a household thang.

5. Cold-Filtered H20 (Free-verse)

Look at this friend.
Flying, fair, figurine, floopy, food.
Starring out the window in line,
Watching the dogs go by in time,
Eating, sleeping, and gossiping.
Five dogs walk by in one day.
Security Camera sees and catches them all in the window.
Is dog watching normal?
How much is the dog in the window?
Fur(r)y.

6. My Childhood Art

zzzzzz

xxxxxx

x xxx

x x x x

x x x x x x

x x. x x x

xxx. xx. xxx

x xx x x

x xxxxx.

xxxx.

!

7. Ice Cream (Free-verse)

Believe in adventure.

Goodie-2-shoes, goofy, guttural, gutsy, glad.

She sits in the car with a seat-belt, *age 5 y/o*,

Screaming one-liners with no pelt.

Wind to be felt.

She was born two weeks after the President's speech.

Her birth was planned — super-breeder.

Is she better?

Is she smarter!?

Wee!

8. Facebook ...?

Hi Jessica, are you still on facebook?

This line was published to me in email. One day in June or July 2024. I just re-read the email now, and it made me think. I am not on Facebook.

If we are all called to be seen, what if we choose to be absent?

So existential.

Sorry Zuckerberg.

9. Liquid (Free-Verse)

My friend has two views.
Dumb and dumber, do-little and be-cool, dangerous and
nice, Dunkin' and Duke, designer and brat.
Opposites — kinda,
Big and small, red and blue — kinda,
They are well-trained. (No they are.)
Both nap after they eat.
Both listen and respond to commands.
One can answer for the other, right!?
Of course, they are in symbiosis!?
Duplicity.

1. Ramblings of the Day with a Dog

The point of self-reflection is not to sit around sounding esoteric or try and be smart, but it is to understand self -- so much -- that we can forge relationships and affect, create, assist, and build us, others, and society. That is everyone's goal.

As I logged off-line, I thought to myself – I don't know my own space. I looked in the mirror and applied makeup and took a piece of candy out of my secret spot and withdrew. I am not jealous of being younger or the younger generation, but I am jealous of the past. I feel invisible. I used to be hip and cute -- not anymore. That's easy to think about but hard to accept.

If any of this sounds familiar, then welcome to the 40's of a spinster. I called my long-lost friend the day before; I check that box. I went to the grocery store last week; I check that box. I got a lot done. I reached out to a few professional contacts on my on-going, seemingly never-ending job search, and I got that done. I prayed to my Saint, and I felt good. I got that done.

Days seemed a bit dry. I hadn't had a drink in about five-years, and I was in an alienating relationship. That was a tale to tell. They have said every new day is a new choice, and every new second is a new hope, but that seemed very optimistic. How can the longing for being young really move you in the direction of hope when the reality tells you that the hope lies in the past.

I heard a bark.

"Sooo...."

11. Frozen - (Free-Verse)

The tail wags the dog.
What, why, who, where, when, whoa
—> whiskey.
If I take a seat to be and see,
Who will join me!?
Depends on the journey!
I never understood that phrase.
Its very complex.
Does it deal with money!?
A dog has a tail and it wags first!?
Troubling!

12. Dad's Haiku

Haiku 1

Dad ate a big meal,

Silent words staying put.

Swallow; no speaking.

Haiku 2

Now it's time to sleep,

To be a Leader seems so blue.

Pacing kindly now.

Haiku 3

Soon it's the day's end.

Kind heart sleeping lay.

Palpitations end.

13. Frost (Free-verse)

The time spent on the computer is hard.

Pinch, punch, puke, pat, pick, pine, pin, pat.

I stare at the screen,

The screen stares at me.

Is the camera on?

I never thought writing was so hard.

I realized writing was hard when it was a mirror for thought.

Why do we punch keys to speak?

Can my mind stop racing!?

Fright.

14. Ballad

[empty] [empty] [empty] [empty] [empty]
[empty] [empty] [empty] [empty] [empty]
[empty] [empty] [empty] [empty] [empty]
[empty] [empty] [empty] [empty] [empty]
[empty] [empty] [empty] [empty] [empty]

[empty] [empty] [empty] [empty] [empty]
[empty] [empty] [empty] [empty] [empty]
[empty] [empty] [empty] [empty] [empty]
[empty] [empty] [empty] [empty] [empty]
[empty] [empty] [empty] [empty] [empty]

[empty] [empty] [empty] [empty] [empty]
[empty] [empty] [empty] [empty] [empty]
[empty] [empty] [empty] [empty] [empty]
[empty] [empty] [empty] [empty] [empty]
[empty] [empty] [empty] [empty] [empty]

[empty] [empty] [empty] [empty] [empty]
[empty] [empty] [empty] [empty] [empty]
[empty] [empty] [empty] [empty] [empty]
[empty] [empty] [empty] [empty] [empty]
[empty] [empty] [empty] [empty] [empty]

[empty] [empty] [empty] [empty] [empty]
[empty] [empty] [empty] [empty] [empty]
[empty] [empty] [empty] [empty] [empty]
[empty] [empty] [empty] [empty] [empty]
[empty] [empty] [empty] [empty] [empty]

[empty] [empty] [empty] [empty] [empty]
[empty] [empty] [empty] [empty] [empty]
[empty] [empty] [empty] [empty] [empty]
[empty] [empty] [empty] [empty] [empty]
[empty] [empty] [empty] [empty] [empty]

[empty] [empty] [empty] [empty] [empty]
[empty] [empty] [empty] [empty] [empty]
[empty] [empty] [empty] [empty] [empty]
[empty] [empty] [empty] [empty] [empty]
[empty] [empty] [empty] [empty] [empty]

[empty] [empty] [empty] [empty] [empty]
[empty] [empty] [empty] [empty] [empty]
[empty] [empty] [empty] [empty] [empty]
[empty] [empty] [empty] [empty] [empty]
[empty] [empty] [empty] [empty] [empty]

[empty] [empty] [empty] [empty] [empty]
[empty] [empty] [empty] [empty] [empty]
[empty] [empty] [empty] [empty] [empty]

[empty] [empty] [empty] [empty] [empty]
[empty] [empty] [empty] [empty] [empty]

<Fill in with favorite song. To be done.>

15. Sweat - (Free-verse)

It takes longer to walk with a puppy.
Dodging DOGE, dogging, dashing, dancing, doin',
dreamin'
I walk to get a better view of earth.
Earth stares back — so worth (it).
Such an existential birth.
I used to be able to walk and read.
Now, I read and walk.
Hi, what's the moon's name!!?
Awww, so cute!
Worldy.

16. Be.I.ng

L.I.F.E. means smiling for the camera.

L.I.F.E. means not quitting when the chips are down.

L.I.F.E. means be.i.ng.

L.I.F.E. means accepting friends as they come and go into your life.

Love Your L.I.F.E.

It's adaptation.

17. Mixer (Free-verse)

I never intend to order for you.
Spacey, spooky, silly, sly, sautéed, saucy.
You only like chicken? - such a carnivore!
When I boil it down — it's such a bore.
Cooking it in micro cuts the chore.
I never ever will pay $80 a week for this specialized
eating plan or diet.
They said it has four legs at birth.
I heard eggs are 400% more expensive this week.
Let's leave them out. Tariff - ica !
Blessed!

18. Face Plant

$h343 onc3 w19 1 dog who could dine,
Who wo43 1 9m1ll h1$ 1nd n!c3 mine.
H3'd $w!4l 1nd h3'd lose,
W!$h 1 ch334ful w!d3 choose,
1nd h3 ch14m3d 1ll $h3 folk9 w!$h h!9 fine.

$h343 onc3 w19 1 dog f4om bing,
Who93 fu4 w19 1 d1&&l3d m!x of yahoo.
H3 lov3d $o ch193 c1$9,
1nd w314 funny h1$9,
Wh!l3 howl!ng 1 $un3ful "Googl3!"

On3 d1y 19 h3 look3d fo4 9om3 fun,
H3 9&o$$3d 1 4122!$ on $h3 run.
W!$h 1 ju2!l1n$ 214k,
H3 41c3d $h4ough $h3 &14k,
Und34n31$h $h3 w14m 9umm34 pun.

9o h3 91$ w!$h 1 9!gh 1nd 1 beggin,
$h!nk!ng of $h3 n3x$ d1y h3'd friggin,
W!$h h!9 $1!l w1gg!ng 1000k.
H3 l3$ $h3 $!m3 goose-eg0,
D431m!ng of 1dv3n$u439 digging.

19. Pause (Free-verse)

I saw five leaves on the ground today.
Bounce, bite, boom, buoyancy, bash.
I never understood the pulling,
such grinding and dragging.
It's hard to be charming.
Dog goes on three walks a day.
All monitored by me.
It's not that sexy!
It's not that fun!
Wishing!

20. Epilogue and Thanks!

Thanks so much for reading this book of poems. I wanted to share a few thoughts on my process.

First, thank you to Book Leaf Publishing for the opportunity — I entered and wrote as part of a writing contest and while the 21-day timeline was short, the publishing opportunity is immensely worth-while.

I personally love poetry as it is lyrical and dream-like but when you try to write it — "oh, is it hard." I didn't really have a plan for this book, but if you are writing modern poetry, you have to play form off of function. And it is hard to balance theme with creativity.

If I could do the 21-day challenge over, I would recommend it to everyone as long as you have some time as the writing is hard. Like three hours a day. You also cannot let perfection or perfectionism in writing get to you. I would recommend you brainstorm a topic or theme and then implement.

And, if you don't like it, delete and start again.

www.ingramcontent.com/pod-product-compliance
Lightning Source LLC
LaVergne TN
LVHW021340200726
843509LV00014B/2601